AF191914

This Logbook belongs to:

_____

_____

Golf life

Impressions and Reviews

≡Capentum

Golf life.
Impressions and Reviews

Editor Mats Lindh
Translation by Robert North
First edition.
Copyright © Capentum Förlag, 2020
All rights reserved. No part of this book may be used or reproduced in any manner whatsoever without written permission except in the case of brief quotations embodied in critical articles or reviews.

Published by Capentum Förlag, Sweden.
Printed by BoD, Norderstedt, Germany, 2020

ISBN 978-91-985341-5-3

www.capentum.com

Best golfer!

This is a book that over time becomes increasingly valuable based on the memories and experiences that you choose to write yourself. The value of being able to look back and remember which golf courses and games have been rewarding is always a good starting point, especially when it is time to plan for new golf trips.

Here in ready made templates, you can add your own notes about dates, current course, number of strokes and scores, and who you played with or met on the course. In addition, you can also rate the actual club's conditions on the basis of a score scale between 1-5 points, and then be able to make interesting comparisons with other visited courses.

Our hope is that you will get a rewarding use of this logbook as a good reminder based on your golf trips.

Have a good golf life.

CONTENT

Golf Club / City	Date	Point	Page

© Capentum Förlag

CONTENT

Golf course / City	Date	Point	Page

© Capentum Förlag

Golf club

Name of the club:					Date	☐ First visit ☐ Return visit		
Address:					Lodging	Distance	Price	
GPS:					Hotel ☐			
Website:					Cabin ☐			
Pay and Play ☐ Yes ☐ No	Short hole course ☐ Yes ☐ No	Name benefit card	Price		RV park ☐			
Golf package ☐ Yes ☐ No	Handigolf ☐ Yes ☐ No	Footgolf ☐ Yes ☐ No	Discount		Other ☐			

☐ Courses (1-5p) (Location, environment, maintenance, accessibility etc.)

☐ Facilities (1-5p) (Standard on toilets, showers, dressing room, lodging, parking etc.)

☐ Service (1-5p) (Service from staff, info material, booking, shops, restaurants, wifi access etc.)

☐ Total (max 15p)

© Capentum Förlag

Game activity

The most positive / negative with this golf club and its courses

Number of holes	Training with lighting	Driving range ok	Price worthy	Want to return
☐ 9 ☐ 18 ☐ 27 ☐ 36	☐ Yes ☐ No	☐ Yes ☐ No	☐ Yes ☐ No	☐ Yes ☐ No

Played from tee:	Winter greens	Handicap qualifying rounds possible	Open all year around
☐ White ☐ Yellow ☐ Blue ☐ Red	☐ Yes ☐ No	☐ Yes ☐ No	☐ Yes ☐ No

Date	Strokes	Scores	Played with:

Golf club

| Name of the club: | Date | ☐ First visit |
| | | ☐ Return visit |

		Lodging	Distance	Price
Address:				
GPS:		Hotel ☐		
Website:		Cabin ☐		

Pay and Play ☐ Yes ☐ No	Short hole course ☐ Yes ☐ No	Name benefit card	Price	RV park ☐		
Golf package ☐ Yes ☐ No	Handigolf ☐ Yes ☐ No	Footgolf ☐ Yes ☐ No	Discount	Other ☐		

☐ Courses (1-5p) (Location, environment, maintenance, accessibility etc.)

☐ Facilities   (1-5p) (Standard on toilets, showers, dressing room, lodging, parking etc.)

☐ Service (1-5p) (Service from staff, info material, booking, shops, restaurants, wifi access etc.)

☐ Total (max 15p)

© Capentum Förlag

Game activity

The most positive / negative with this golf club and its courses

Number of holes				Training with lighting		Driving range ok		Price worthy		Want to return	
☐ 9	☐ 18	☐ 27	☐ 36	☐ Yes	☐ No	☐ Yes	☐ No	☐ Yes	☐ No	☐ Yes	☐ No

Played from tee:				Winter greens		Handicap qualifying rounds possible		Open all year around	
☐ White	☐ Yellow	☐ Blue	☐ Red	☐ Yes	☐ No	☐ Yes	☐ No	☐ Yes	☐ No

Date	Strokes	Scores	Played with:

Golf club

Name of the club:		Date	☐ First visit ☐ Return visit	
Address:		Lodging	Distance	Price
GPS:		Hotel ☐		
Website:		Cabin ☐		

Pay and Play ☐ Yes ☐ No	Short hole course ☐ Yes ☐ No	Name benefit card	Price	RV park ☐		
Golf package ☐ Yes ☐ No	Handigolf ☐ Yes ☐ No	Footgolf ☐ Yes ☐ No	Discount	Other ☐		

☐ Courses (1-5p) (Location, environment, maintenance, accessibility etc.)

☐ Facilities   (1-5p) (Standard on toilets, showers, dressing room, lodging, parking etc.)

☐ Service (1-5p) (Service from staff, info material, booking, shops, restaurants, wifi access etc.)

☐ Total (max 15p)

© Capentum Förlag

Game activity

The most positive / negative with this golf club and its courses

Number of holes	Training with lighting	Driving range ok	Price worthy	Want to return
☐ 9 ☐ 18 ☐ 27 ☐ 36	☐ Yes ☐ No	☐ Yes ☐ No	☐ Yes ☐ No	☐ Yes ☐ No

Played from tee:	Winter greens	Handicap qualifying rounds possible	Open all year around
☐ White ☐ Yellow ☐ Blue ☐ Red	☐ Yes ☐ No	☐ Yes ☐ No	☐ Yes ☐ No

Date	Strokes	Scores	Played with:

Golf club

Name of the club:					Date	☐ First visit ☐ Return visit		
Address:					Lodging	Distance	Price	
GPS:					Hotel ☐			
Website:					Cabin ☐			
Pay and Play ☐ Yes ☐ No	Short hole course ☐ Yes ☐ No	Name benefit card		Price	RV park ☐			
Golf package ☐ Yes ☐ No	Handigolf ☐ Yes ☐ No	Footgolf ☐ Yes ☐ No		Discount	Other ☐			

☐ Courses (1-5p) (Location, environment, maintenance, accessibility etc.)

☐ Facilities (1-5p) (Standard on toilets, showers, dressing room, lodging, parking etc.)

☐ Service (1-5p) (Service from staff, info material, booking, shops, restaurants, wifi access etc.)

☐ Total (max 15p)

Ⓒ Capentum Förlag

Game activity

The most positive / negative with this golf club and its courses

Number of holes				Training with lighting		Driving range ok		Price worthy		Want to return	
☐ 9	☐ 18	☐ 27	☐ 36	☐ Yes	☐ No	☐ Yes	☐ No	☐ Yes	☐ No	☐ Yes	☐ No

Played from tee:				Winter greens		Handicap qualifying rounds possible		Open all year around	
☐ White	☐ Yellow	☐ Blue	☐ Red	☐ Yes	☐ No	☐ Yes	☐ No	☐ Yes	☐ No

Date	Strokes	Scores	Played with:

Golf club

Name of the club:					Date	First visit
						Return visit

Address:	Lodging	Distance	Price
GPS:	Hotel ☐		
Website:	Cabin ☐		

Pay and Play	Short hole course	Name benefit card	Price	RV park
☐ Yes ☐ No	☐ Yes ☐ No			☐
Golf package	Handigolf	Footgolf	Discount	Other
☐ Yes ☐ No	☐ Yes ☐ No	☐ Yes ☐ No		☐

☐ Courses (1–5p) (Location, environment, maintenance, accessibility etc.)

☐ Facilities (1–5p) (Standard on toilets, showers, dressing room, lodging, parking etc.)

☐ Service (1–5p) (Service from staff, info material, booking, shops, restaurants, wifi access etc.)

☐ Total (max 15p)

© Capentum Förlag

Game activity

The most positive / negative with this golf club and its courses

Number of holes	Training with lighting	Driving range ok	Price worthy	Want to return
☐ 9 ☐ 18 ☐ 27 ☐ 36	☐ Yes ☐ No	☐ Yes ☐ No	☐ Yes ☐ No	☐ Yes ☐ No

Played from tee:	Winter greens	Handicap qualifying rounds possible	Open all year around
☐ White ☐ Yellow ☐ Blue ☐ Red	☐ Yes ☐ No	☐ Yes ☐ No	☐ Yes ☐ No

Date	Strokes	Scores	Played with:

Golf club

Name of the club:					Date	☐ First visit ☐ Return visit		
Address:					Lodging	Distance	Price	
GPS:					Hotel ☐			
Website:					Cabin ☐			

Pay and Play ☐ Yes ☐ No	Short hole course ☐ Yes ☐ No	Name benefit card	Price	RV park ☐
Golf package ☐ Yes ☐ No	Handigolf ☐ Yes ☐ No	Footgolf ☐ Yes ☐ No	Discount	Other ☐

☐ **Courses (1–5p)** (Location, environment, maintenance, accessibility etc.)

☐ **Facilities (1–5p)** (Standard on toilets, showers, dressing room, lodging, parking etc.)

☐ **Service (1–5p)** (Service from staff, info material, booking, shops, restaurants, wifi access etc.)

☐ Total (max 15p)

© Capentum Förlag

Game activity

The most positive / negative with this golf club and its courses

Number of holes				Training with lighting		Driving range ok		Price worthy		Want to return	
☐ 9 ☐ 18 ☐ 27 ☐ 36				☐ Yes ☐ No		☐ Yes ☐ No		☐ Yes ☐ No		☐ Yes ☐ No	

Played from tee:				Winter greens		Handicap qualifying rounds possible		Open all year around	
☐ White ☐ Yellow ☐ Blue ☐ Red				☐ Yes ☐ No		☐ Yes ☐ No		☐ Yes ☐ No	

Date	Strokes	Scores	Played with:

Golf club

		Date	First visit ☐ Return visit ☐		
Name of the club:					
Address:		Lodging	Distance		Price
GPS:		Hotel ☐			
Website:		Cabin ☐			

Pay and Play ☐ Yes ☐ No	Short hole course ☐ Yes ☐ No	Name benefit card	Price	RV park ☐	
Golf package ☐ Yes ☐ No	Handigolf ☐ Yes ☐ No	Footgolf ☐ Yes ☐ No	Discount	Other ☐	

☐ **Courses** (1-5p) (Location, environment, maintenance, accessibility etc.)

☐ **Facilities** (1-5p) (Standard on toilets, showers, dressing room, lodging, parking etc.)

☐ **Service** (1-5p) (Service from staff, info material, booking, shops, restaurants, wifi access etc.)

☐ **Total** (max 15p)

Ⓒ Capentum Förlag

Game activity

The most positive / negative with this golf club and its courses

Number of holes	Training with lighting	Driving range ok	Price worthy	Want to return
☐ 9 ☐ 18 ☐ 27 ☐ 36	☐ Yes ☐ No	☐ Yes ☐ No	☐ Yes ☐ No	☐ Yes ☐ No

Played from tee:	Winter greens	Handicap qualifying rounds possible	Open all year around
☐ White ☐ Yellow ☐ Blue ☐ Red	☐ Yes ☐ No	☐ Yes ☐ No	☐ Yes ☐ No

Date	Strokes	Scores	Played with:

Golf club

Name of the club:		Date	First visit ☐
			Return visit ☐

Address:	Lodging	Distance	Price
GPS:	Hotel ☐		
Website:	Cabin ☐		

Pay and Play ☐ Yes ☐ No	Short hole course ☐ Yes ☐ No	Name benefit card	Price	RV park ☐		
Golf package ☐ Yes ☐ No	Handigolf ☐ Yes ☐ No	Footgolf ☐ Yes ☐ No	Discount	Other ☐		

☐ Courses (1–5p) (Location, environment, maintenance, accessibility etc.)

☐ Facilities (1–5p) (Standard on toilets, showers, dressing room, lodging, parking etc.)

☐ Service (1–5p) (Service from staff, info material, booking, shops, restaurants, wifi access etc.)

☐ Total (max 15p)

© Capentum Förlag

Game activity

The most positive / negative with this golf club and its courses

Number of holes	Training with lighting	Driving range ok	Price worthy	Want to return
☐ 9 ☐ 18 ☐ 27 ☐ 36	☐ Yes ☐ No	☐ Yes ☐ No	☐ Yes ☐ No	☐ Yes ☐ No

Played from tee:	Winter greens	Handicap qualifying rounds possible	Open all year around
☐ White ☐ Yellow ☐ Blue ☐ Red	☐ Yes ☐ No	☐ Yes ☐ No	☐ Yes ☐ No

Date	Strokes	Scores	Played with:

Golf club

Name of the club:					Date	First visit ☐		
						Return visit ☐		
Address:					Lodging	Distance	Price	
GPS:					Hotel ☐			
Website:					Cabin ☐			

Pay and Play	Short hole course	Name benefit card	Price	RV park		
☐ Yes ☐ No	☐ Yes ☐ No			☐		
Golf package	Handigolf	Footgolf	Discount	Other		
☐ Yes ☐ No	☐ Yes ☐ No	☐ Yes ☐ No		☐		

☐ Courses (1-5p) (Location, environment, maintenance, accessibility etc.)

☐ Facilities (1-5p) (Standard on toilets, showers, dressing room, lodging, parking etc.)

☐ Service (1-5p) (Service from staff, info material, booking, shops, restaurants, wifi access etc.)

☐ Total (max 15p)

© Capentum Förlag

Game activity

The most positive / negative with this golf club and its courses

Number of holes	Training with lighting	Driving range ok	Price worthy	Want to return
☐ 9 ☐ 18 ☐ 27 ☐ 36	☐ Yes ☐ No	☐ Yes ☐ No	☐ Yes ☐ No	☐ Yes ☐ No

Played from tee:	Winter greens	Handicap qualifying rounds possible	Open all year around
☐ White ☐ Yellow ☐ Blue ☐ Red	☐ Yes ☐ No	☐ Yes ☐ No	☐ Yes ☐ No

Date	Strokes	Scores	Played with:

Golf club

Name of the club:		Date	First visit ☐
			Return visit ☐

Address:		Lodging	Distance	Price
GPS:		Hotel ☐		
Website:		Cabin ☐		

Pay and Play	Short hole course	Name benefit card	Price	RV park ☐		
☐ Yes ☐ No	☐ Yes ☐ No					
Golf package	Handigolf	Footgolf	Discount	Other ☐		
☐ Yes ☐ No	☐ Yes ☐ No	☐ Yes ☐ No				

☐ **Courses (1–5p)** (Location, environment, maintenance, accessibility etc.)

☐ **Facilities (1–5p)** (Standard on toilets, showers, dressing room, lodging, parking etc.)

☐ **Service (1–5p)** (Service from staff, info material, booking, shops, restaurants, wifi access etc.)

☐ Total (max 15p)

© Capentum Förlag

Game activity

The most positive / negative with this golf club and its courses

Number of holes	Training with lighting	Driving range ok	Price worthy	Want to return
☐ 9 ☐ 18 ☐ 27 ☐ 36	☐ Yes ☐ No	☐ Yes ☐ No	☐ Yes ☐ No	☐ Yes ☐ No

Played from tee:	Winter greens	Handicap qualifying rounds possible	Open all year around
☐ White ☐ Yellow ☐ Blue ☐ Red	☐ Yes ☐ No	☐ Yes ☐ No	☐ Yes ☐ No

Date	Strokes	Scores	Played with:

Golf club

Name of the club:					Date		☐ First visit
							☐ Return visit

Address:	Lodging	Distance	Price

GPS:	Hotel ☐		

Website:	Cabin ☐		

Pay and Play ☐ Yes ☐ No	Short hole course ☐ Yes ☐ No	Name benefit card	Price	RV park ☐		
Golf package ☐ Yes ☐ No	Handigolf ☐ Yes ☐ No	Footgolf ☐ Yes ☐ No	Discount	Other ☐		

☐ Courses (1-5p) (Location, environment, maintenance, accessibility etc.)

☐ Facilities (1-5p) (Standard on toilets, showers, dressing room, lodging, parking etc.)

☐ Service (1-5p) (Service from staff, info material, booking, shops, restaurants, wifi access etc.)

☐ Total (max 15p)

© Capentum Förlag

Game activity

The most positive / negative with this golf club and its courses

Number of holes	Training with lighting	Driving range ok	Price worthy	Want to return
☐ 9 ☐ 18 ☐ 27 ☐ 36	☐ Yes ☐ No	☐ Yes ☐ No	☐ Yes ☐ No	☐ Yes ☐ No

Played from tee:	Winter greens	Handicap qualifying rounds possible	Open all year around
☐ White ☐ Yellow ☐ Blue ☐ Red	☐ Yes ☐ No	☐ Yes ☐ No	☐ Yes ☐ No

Date	Strokes	Scores	Played with:

Golf club

Name of the club:			Date	First visit ☐ Return visit ☐		
Address:			Lodging		Distance	Price
GPS:			Hotel ☐			
Website:			Cabin ☐			

Pay and Play ☐ Yes ☐ No	Short hole course ☐ Yes ☐ No	Name benefit card	Price	RV park ☐		
Golf package ☐ Yes ☐ No	Handigolf ☐ Yes ☐ No	Footgolf ☐ Yes ☐ No	Discount	Other ☐		

☐ Courses (1–5p) (Location, environment, maintenance, accessibility etc.)

☐ Facilities (1–5p) (Standard on toilets, showers, dressing room, lodging, parking etc.)

☐ Service (1–5p) (Service from staff, info material, booking, shops, restaurants, wifi access etc.)

☐ Total (max 15p)

© Capentum Förlag

Game activity

The most positive / negative with this golf club and its courses

Number of holes	Training with lighting	Driving range ok	Price worthy	Want to return
☐ 9 ☐ 18 ☐ 27 ☐ 36	☐ Yes ☐ No	☐ Yes ☐ No	☐ Yes ☐ No	☐ Yes ☐ No

Played from tee:	Winter greens	Handicap qualifying rounds possible	Open all year around
☐ White ☐ Yellow ☐ Blue ☐ Red	☐ Yes ☐ No	☐ Yes ☐ No	☐ Yes ☐ No

Date	Strokes	Scores	Played with:

Golf club

Name of the club:				Date	☐ First visit ☐ Return visit		
Address:				Lodging	Distance	Price	
GPS:				Hotel ☐			
Website:				Cabin ☐			

Pay and Play ☐ Yes ☐ No	Short hole course ☐ Yes ☐ No	Name benefit card	Price	RV park ☐		
Golf package ☐ Yes ☐ No	Handigolf ☐ Yes ☐ No	Footgolf ☐ Yes ☐ No	Discount	Other ☐		

☐ Courses (1-5p) (Location, environment, maintenance, accessibility etc.)

☐ Facilities (1-5p) (Standard on toilets, showers, dressing room, lodging, parking etc.)

☐ Service (1-5p) (Service from staff, info material, booking, shops, restaurants, wifi access etc.)

☐ Total (max 15p)

© Capentum Förlag

Game activity

The most positive / negative with this golf club and its courses

Number of holes				Training with lighting		Driving range ok		Price worthy		Want to return	
☐ 9	☐ 18	☐ 27	☐ 36	☐ Yes	☐ No	☐ Yes	☐ No	☐ Yes	☐ No	☐ Yes	☐ No

Played from tee:				Winter greens		Handicap qualifying rounds possible		Open all year around	
☐ White	☐ Yellow	☐ Blue	☐ Red	☐ Yes	☐ No	☐ Yes	☐ No	☐ Yes	☐ No

Date	Strokes	Scores	Played with:

Golf club

| Name of the club: | Date | ☐ First visit |
| | | ☐ Return visit |

Name of the club:		Date		First visit
				Return visit

Address:	Lodging	Distance	Price
GPS:	Hotel ☐		
Website:	Cabin ☐		

Pay and Play ☐ Yes ☐ No	Short hole course ☐ Yes ☐ No	Name benefit card	Price	RV park ☐		
Golf package ☐ Yes ☐ No	Handigolf ☐ Yes ☐ No	Footgolf ☐ Yes ☐ No	Discount	Other ☐		

☐ Courses (1-5p) (Location, environment, maintenance, accessibility etc.)

☐ Facilities   (1-5p) (Standard on toilets, showers, dressing room, lodging, parking etc.)

☐ Service (1-5p) (Service from staff, info material, booking, shops, restaurants, wifi access etc.)

☐ Total (max 15p)

© Capentum Förlag

Game activity

The most positive / negative with this golf club and its courses

Number of holes				Training with lighting		Driving range ok		Price worthy		Want to return	
☐ 9	☐ 18	☐ 27	☐ 36	☐ Yes	☐ No	☐ Yes	☐ No	☐ Yes	☐ No	☐ Yes	☐ No

Played from tee:				Winter greens		Handicap qualifying rounds possible		Open all year around	
☐ White	☐ Yellow	☐ Blue	☐ Red	☐ Yes	☐ No	☐ Yes	☐ No	☐ Yes	☐ No

Date	Strokes	Scores	Played with:

Golf club

Name of the club:				Date	First visit ☐ / Return visit ☐	

Address:		Lodging	Distance	Price
GPS:		Hotel ☐		
Website:		Cabin ☐		

Pay and Play ☐ Yes ☐ No	Short hole course ☐ Yes ☐ No	Name benefit card	Price	RV park ☐		
Golf package ☐ Yes ☐ No	Handigolf ☐ Yes ☐ No	Footgolf ☐ Yes ☐ No	Discount	Other ☐		

☐ Courses (1-5p) (Location, environment, maintenance, accessibility etc.)

☐ Facilities (1-5p) (Standard on toilets, showers, dressing room, lodging, parking etc.)

☐ Service (1-5p) (Service from staff, info material, booking, shops, restaurants, wifi access etc.)

☐ Total (max 15p)

Ⓒ Capentum Förlag

Game activity

The most positive / negative with this golf club and its courses

Number of holes	Training with lighting	Driving range ok	Price worthy	Want to return
☐ 9 ☐ 18 ☐ 27 ☐ 36	☐ Yes ☐ No	☐ Yes ☐ No	☐ Yes ☐ No	☐ Yes ☐ No

Played from tee:	Winter greens	Handicap qualifying rounds possible	Open all year around
☐ White ☐ Yellow ☐ Blue ☐ Red	☐ Yes ☐ No	☐ Yes ☐ No	☐ Yes ☐ No

Date	Strokes	Scores	Played with:

Golf club

Name of the club:					Date	☐ First visit ☐ Return visit	

Address:					Lodging	Distance	Price
GPS:					Hotel ☐		
Website:					Cabin ☐		

Pay and Play ☐ Yes ☐ No	Short hole course ☐ Yes ☐ No	Name benefit card	Price	RV park ☐		
Golf package ☐ Yes ☐ No	Handigolf ☐ Yes ☐ No	Footgolf ☐ Yes ☐ No	Discount	Other ☐		

☐ **Courses** (1-5p) (Location, environment, maintenance, accessibility etc.)

☐ **Facilities** (1-5p) (Standard on toilets, showers, dressing room, lodging, parking etc.)

☐ **Service** (1-5p) (Service from staff, info material, booking, shops, restaurants, wifi access etc.)

☐ **Total** (max 15p)

© Capentum Förlag

Game activity

The most positive / negative with this golf club and its courses

Number of holes	Training with lighting	Driving range ok	Price worthy	Want to return
☐ 9 ☐ 18 ☐ 27 ☐ 36	☐ Yes ☐ No	☐ Yes ☐ No	☐ Yes ☐ No	☐ Yes ☐ No

Played from tee:	Winter greens	Handicap qualifying rounds possible	Open all year around
☐ White ☐ Yellow ☐ Blue ☐ Red	☐ Yes ☐ No	☐ Yes ☐ No	☐ Yes ☐ No

Date	Strokes	Scores	Played with:

Golf club

Name of the club:	Date	☐ First visit
		☐ Return visit

	Lodging	Distance	Price
Address:			
GPS:	Hotel ☐		
Website:	Cabin ☐		

Pay and Play ☐ Yes ☐ No	Short hole course ☐ Yes ☐ No	Name benefit card	Price	RV park ☐		
Golf package ☐ Yes ☐ No	Handigolf ☐ Yes ☐ No	Footgolf ☐ Yes ☐ No	Discount	Other ☐		

☐ Courses (1-5p) (Location, environment, maintenance, accessibility etc.)

☐ Facilities (1-5p) (Standard on toilets, showers, dressing room, lodging, parking etc.)

☐ Service (1-5p) (Service from staff, info material, booking, shops, restaurants, wifi access etc.)

☐ Total (max 15p)

© Capentum Förlag

Game activity

The most positive / negative with this golf club and its courses

Number of holes	Training with lighting	Driving range ok	Price worthy	Want to return
☐ 9 ☐ 18 ☐ 27 ☐ 36	☐ Yes ☐ No	☐ Yes ☐ No	☐ Yes ☐ No	☐ Yes ☐ No

Played from tee:	Winter greens	Handicap qualifying rounds possible	Open all year around
☐ White ☐ Yellow ☐ Blue ☐ Red	☐ Yes ☐ No	☐ Yes ☐ No	☐ Yes ☐ No

Date	Strokes	Scores	Played with:

Golf club

Name of the club:					Date	☐ First visit ☐ Return visit		
Address:					Lodging	Distance	Price	
GPS:					Hotel ☐			
Website:					Cabin ☐			

Pay and Play ☐ Yes ☐ No	Short hole course ☐ Yes ☐ No	Name benefit card	Price	RV park ☐		
Golf package ☐ Yes ☐ No	Handigolf ☐ Yes ☐ No	Footgolf ☐ Yes ☐ No	Discount	Other ☐		

☐ Courses (1-5p) (Location, environment, maintenance, accessibility etc.)

☐ Facilities (1-5p) (Standard on toilets, showers, dressing room, lodging, parking etc.)

☐ Service (1-5p) (Service from staff, info material, booking, shops, restaurants, wifi access etc.)

☐ Total (max 15p)

Ⓒ Capentum Förlag

Game activity

The most positive / negative with this golf club and its courses

Number of holes	Training with lighting	Driving range ok	Price worthy	Want to return
☐ 9 ☐ 18 ☐ 27 ☐ 36	☐ Yes ☐ No	☐ Yes ☐ No	☐ Yes ☐ No	☐ Yes ☐ No

Played from tee:	Winter greens	Handicap qualifying rounds possible	Open all year around
☐ White ☐ Yellow ☐ Blue ☐ Red	☐ Yes ☐ No	☐ Yes ☐ No	☐ Yes ☐ No

Date	Strokes	Scores	Played with:

Golf club

Name of the club:		Date	First visit
			Return visit

Address:		Lodging	Distance	Price
GPS:		Hotel ☐		
Website:		Cabin ☐		

Pay and Play ☐ Yes ☐ No	Short hole course ☐ Yes ☐ No	Name benefit card	Price	RV park ☐		
Golf package ☐ Yes ☐ No	Handigolf ☐ Yes ☐ No	Footgolf ☐ Yes ☐ No	Discount	Other ☐		

☐ Courses (1-5p) (Location, environment, maintenance, accessibility etc.)

☐ Facilities (1-5p) (Standard on toilets, showers, dressing room, lodging, parking etc.)

☐ Service (1-5p) (Service from staff, info material, booking, shops, restaurants, wifi access etc.)

☐ Total (max 15p)

© Capentum Förlag

Game activity

The most positive / negative with this golf club and its courses

Number of holes	Training with lighting	Driving range ok	Price worthy	Want to return
☐ 9 ☐ 18 ☐ 27 ☐ 36	☐ Yes ☐ No	☐ Yes ☐ No	☐ Yes ☐ No	☐ Yes ☐ No

Played from tee:	Winter greens	Handicap qualifying rounds possible	Open all year around
☐ White ☐ Yellow ☐ Blue ☐ Red	☐ Yes ☐ No	☐ Yes ☐ No	☐ Yes ☐ No

Date	Strokes	Scores	Played with:

Golf club

| Name of the club: | Date | First visit |
| | | Return visit |

| Address: | | Lodging | Distance | Price |

| GPS: | Hotel ☐ | | |

| Website: | Cabin ☐ | | |

| Pay and Play ☐ Yes ☐ No | Short hole course ☐ Yes ☐ No | Name benefit card | Price | RV park ☐ | | |
| Golf package ☐ Yes ☐ No | Handigolf ☐ Yes ☐ No | Footgolf ☐ Yes ☐ No | Discount | Other ☐ | | |

☐ Courses (1-5p) (Location, environment, maintenance, accessibility etc.)

☐ Facilities (1-5p) (Standard on toilets, showers, dressing room, lodging, parking etc.)

☐ Service (1-5p) (Service from staff, info material, booking, shops, restaurants, wifi access etc.)

☐ Total (max 15p)

© Capentum Förlag

Game activity

The most positive / negative with this golf club and its courses

Number of holes	Training with lighting	Driving range ok	Price worthy	Want to return
☐ 9 ☐ 18 ☐ 27 ☐ 36	☐ Yes ☐ No	☐ Yes ☐ No	☐ Yes ☐ No	☐ Yes ☐ No

Played from tee:	Winter greens	Handicap qualifying rounds possible	Open all year around
☐ White ☐ Yellow ☐ Blue ☐ Red	☐ Yes ☐ No	☐ Yes ☐ No	☐ Yes ☐ No

Date	Strokes	Scores	Played with:

Golf club

Name of the club:	Date	First visit
		Return visit

Address:	Lodging	Distance	Price
GPS:	Hotel ☐		
Website:	Cabin ☐		

Pay and Play ☐ Yes ☐ No	Short hole course ☐ Yes ☐ No	Name benefit card	Price	RV park ☐
Golf package ☐ Yes ☐ No	Handigolf ☐ Yes ☐ No	Footgolf ☐ Yes ☐ No	Discount	Other ☐

☐ **Courses (1-5p)** (Location, environment, maintenance, accessibility etc.)

☐ **Facilities (1-5p)** (Standard on toilets, showers, dressing room, lodging, parking etc.)

☐ **Service (1-5p)** (Service from staff, info material, booking, shops, restaurants, wifi access etc.)

☐ **Total (max 15p)**

© Capentum Förlag

Game activity

The most positive / negative with this golf club and its courses

Number of holes	Training with lighting	Driving range ok	Price worthy	Want to return
☐ 9 ☐ 18 ☐ 27 ☐ 36	☐ Yes ☐ No	☐ Yes ☐ No	☐ Yes ☐ No	☐ Yes ☐ No

Played from tee:	Winter greens	Handicap qualifying rounds possible	Open all year around
☐ White ☐ Yellow ☐ Blue ☐ Red	☐ Yes ☐ No	☐ Yes ☐ No	☐ Yes ☐ No

Date	Strokes	Scores	Played with:

Golf club

Name of the club:				Date	☐ First visit ☐ Return visit		
Address:				Lodging	Distance	Price	
GPS:				Hotel ☐			
Website:				Cabin ☐			
Pay and Play ☐ Yes ☐ No	Short hole course ☐ Yes ☐ No	Name benefit card	Price	RV park ☐			
Golf package ☐ Yes ☐ No	Handigolf ☐ Yes ☐ No	Footgolf ☐ Yes ☐ No	Discount	Other ☐			

☐ Courses (1-5p) (Location, environment, maintenance, accessibility etc.)

☐ Facilities   (1-5p) (Standard on toilets, showers, dressing room, lodging, parking etc.)

☐ Service (1-5p) (Service from staff, info material, booking, shops, restaurants, wifi access etc.)

☐ Total (max 15p)

© Capentum Förlag

Game activity

The most positive / negative with this golf club and its courses

Number of holes	Training with lighting	Driving range ok	Price worthy	Want to return
☐ 9 ☐ 18 ☐ 27 ☐ 36	☐ Yes ☐ No	☐ Yes ☐ No	☐ Yes ☐ No	☐ Yes ☐ No

Played from tee:	Winter greens	Handicap qualifying rounds possible	Open all year around
☐ White ☐ Yellow ☐ Blue ☐ Red	☐ Yes ☐ No	☐ Yes ☐ No	☐ Yes ☐ No

Date	Strokes	Scores	Played with:

Golf club

Name of the club:				Date	☐ First visit ☐ Return visit	
Address:				Lodging	Distance	Price
GPS:				Hotel ☐		
Website:				Cabin ☐		

Pay and Play ☐ Yes ☐ No	Short hole course ☐ Yes ☐ No	Name benefit card	Price	RV park ☐		
Golf package ☐ Yes ☐ No	Handigolf ☐ Yes ☐ No	Footgolf ☐ Yes ☐ No	Discount	Other ☐		

☐ Courses (1-5p) (Location, environment, maintenance, accessibility etc.)

☐ Facilities (1-5p) (Standard on toilets, showers, dressing room, lodging, parking etc.)

☐ Service (1-5p) (Service from staff, info material, booking, shops, restaurants, wifi access etc.)

☐ Total (max 15p)

© Capentum Förlag

Game activity

The most positive / negative with this golf club and its courses

Number of holes	Training with lighting	Driving range ok	Price worthy	Want to return
☐ 9 ☐ 18 ☐ 27 ☐ 36	☐ Yes ☐ No	☐ Yes ☐ No	☐ Yes ☐ No	☐ Yes ☐ No

Played from tee:	Winter greens	Handicap qualifying rounds possible	Open all year around
☐ White ☐ Yellow ☐ Blue ☐ Red	☐ Yes ☐ No	☐ Yes ☐ No	☐ Yes ☐ No

Date	Strokes	Scores	Played with:

Golf club

Name of the club:			Date	☐ First visit ☐ Return visit	
Address:			Lodging	Distance	Price
GPS:			Hotel ☐		
Website:			Cabin ☐		

Pay and Play ☐ Yes ☐ No	Short hole course ☐ Yes ☐ No	Name benefit card	Price	RV park ☐	
Golf package ☐ Yes ☐ No	Handigolf ☐ Yes ☐ No	Footgolf ☐ Yes ☐ No	Discount	Other ☐	

☐ **Courses** (1-5p) (Location, environment, maintenance, accessibility etc.)

☐ **Facilities**   (1-5p) (Standard on toilets, showers, dressing room, lodging, parking etc.)

☐ **Service** (1-5p) (Service from staff, info material, booking, shops, restaurants, wifi access etc.)

☐ **Total** (max 15p)

© Capentum Förlag

Game activity

The most positive / negative with this golf club and its courses

Number of holes	Training with lighting	Driving range ok	Price worthy	Want to return
☐ 9 ☐ 18 ☐ 27 ☐ 36	☐ Yes ☐ No	☐ Yes ☐ No	☐ Yes ☐ No	☐ Yes ☐ No

Played from tee:	Winter greens	Handicap qualifying rounds possible	Open all year around
☐ White ☐ Yellow ☐ Blue ☐ Red	☐ Yes ☐ No	☐ Yes ☐ No	☐ Yes ☐ No

Date	Strokes	Scores	Played with:

Golf club

Name of the club:				Date	☐ First visit ☐ Return visit		
Address:				Lodging	Distance	Price	
GPS:				Hotel ☐			
Website:				Cabin ☐			

Pay and Play ☐ Yes ☐ No	Short hole course ☐ Yes ☐ No	Name benefit card	Price	RV park ☐		
Golf package ☐ Yes ☐ No	Handigolf ☐ Yes ☐ No	Footgolf ☐ Yes ☐ No	Discount	Other ☐		

☐ Courses (1-5p) (Location, environment, maintenance, accessibility etc.)

☐ Facilities (1-5p) (Standard on toilets, showers, dressing room, lodging, parking etc.)

☐ Service (1-5p) (Service from staff, info material, booking, shops, restaurants, wifi access etc.)

☐ Total (max 15p)

© Capentum Förlag

Game activity

The most positive / negative with this golf club and its courses

Number of holes	Training with lighting	Driving range ok	Price worthy	Want to return
☐ 9 ☐ 18 ☐ 27 ☐ 36	☐ Yes ☐ No	☐ Yes ☐ No	☐ Yes ☐ No	☐ Yes ☐ No

Played from tee:	Winter greens	Handicap qualifying rounds possible	Open all year around
☐ White ☐ Yellow ☐ Blue ☐ Red	☐ Yes ☐ No	☐ Yes ☐ No	☐ Yes ☐ No

Date	Strokes	Scores	Played with:

Golf club

Name of the club:			Date	☐ First visit ☐ Return visit		
Address:			Lodging	Distance	Price	
GPS:			Hotel ☐			
Website:			Cabin ☐			

Pay and Play ☐ Yes ☐ No	Short hole course ☐ Yes ☐ No	Name benefit card	Price	RV park ☐		
Golf package ☐ Yes ☐ No	Handigolf ☐ Yes ☐ No	Footgolf ☐ Yes ☐ No	Discount	Other ☐		

☐ **Courses (1-5p)** (Location, environment, maintenance, accessibility etc.)

☐ **Facilities (1-5p)** (Standard on toilets, showers, dressing room, lodging, parking etc.)

☐ **Service (1-5p)** (Service from staff, info material, booking, shops, restaurants, wifi access etc.)

☐ **Total (max 15p)**

© Capentum Förlag

Game activity

The most positive / negative with this golf club and its courses

Number of holes	Training with lighting	Driving range ok	Price worthy	Want to return
☐ 9 ☐ 18 ☐ 27 ☐ 36	☐ Yes ☐ No	☐ Yes ☐ No	☐ Yes ☐ No	☐ Yes ☐ No

Played from tee:	Winter greens	Handicap qualifying rounds possible	Open all year around
☐ White ☐ Yellow ☐ Blue ☐ Red	☐ Yes ☐ No	☐ Yes ☐ No	☐ Yes ☐ No

Date	Strokes	Scores	Played with:

Golf club

| Name of the club: | Date | ☐ First visit |
| | | ☐ Return visit |

Address:	Lodging	Distance	Price

| GPS: | Hotel ☐ | | |

| Website: | Cabin ☐ | | |

| Pay and Play | Short hole course | Name benefit card | Price | RV park |
| ☐ Yes ☐ No | ☐ Yes ☐ No | | | ☐ |

| Golf package | Handigolf | Footgolf | Discount | Other |
| ☐ Yes ☐ No | ☐ Yes ☐ No | ☐ Yes ☐ No | | ☐ |

☐ **Courses** (1-5p) (Location, environment, maintenance, accessibility etc.)

☐ **Facilities** (1-5p) (Standard on toilets, showers, dressing room, lodging, parking etc.)

☐ **Service** (1-5p) (Service from staff, info material, booking, shops, restaurants, wifi access etc.)

☐ **Total** (max 15p)

© Capentum Förlag

Game activity

The most positive / negative with this golf club and its courses

Number of holes	Training with lighting	Driving range ok	Price worthy	Want to return
☐ 9 ☐ 18 ☐ 27 ☐ 36	☐ Yes ☐ No	☐ Yes ☐ No	☐ Yes ☐ No	☐ Yes ☐ No

Played from tee:	Winter greens	Handicap qualifying rounds possible	Open all year around
☐ White ☐ Yellow ☐ Blue ☐ Red	☐ Yes ☐ No	☐ Yes ☐ No	☐ Yes ☐ No

Date	Strokes	Scores	Played with:

Golf club

Name of the club:				Date	☐ First visit ☐ Return visit		
Address:				Lodging	Distance	Price	
GPS:				Hotel ☐			
Website:				Cabin ☐			

Pay and Play ☐ Yes ☐ No	Short hole course ☐ Yes ☐ No	Name benefit card	Price	RV park ☐		
Golf package ☐ Yes ☐ No	Handigolf ☐ Yes ☐ No	Footgolf ☐ Yes ☐ No	Discount	Other ☐		

☐ **Courses (1-5p)** (Location, environment, maintenance, accessibility etc.)

☐ **Facilities** (1-5p) (Standard on toilets, showers, dressing room, lodging, parking etc.)

☐ **Service** (1-5p) (Service from staff, info material, booking, shops, restaurants, wifi access etc.)

☐ **Total** (max 15p)

© Capentum Förlag

Game activity

The most positive / negative with this golf club and its courses

Number of holes	Training with lighting	Driving range ok	Price worthy	Want to return
☐ 9 ☐ 18 ☐ 27 ☐ 36	☐ Yes ☐ No	☐ Yes ☐ No	☐ Yes ☐ No	☐ Yes ☐ No

Played from tee:	Winter greens	Handicap qualifying rounds possible	Open all year around
☐ White ☐ Yellow ☐ Blue ☐ Red	☐ Yes ☐ No	☐ Yes ☐ No	☐ Yes ☐ No

Date	Strokes	Scores	Played with:

Golf club

Name of the club:	Date	☐ First visit ☐ Return visit		

Address:	Lodging	Distance	Price
GPS:	Hotel ☐		
Website:	Cabin ☐		

Pay and Play ☐ Yes ☐ No	Short hole course ☐ Yes ☐ No	Name benefit card	Price	RV park ☐		
Golf package ☐ Yes ☐ No	Handigolf ☐ Yes ☐ No	Footgolf ☐ Yes ☐ No	Discount	Other ☐		

☐ Courses (1-5p) (Location, environment, maintenance, accessibility etc.)

☐ Facilities (1-5p) (Standard on toilets, showers, dressing room, lodging, parking etc.)

☐ Service (1-5p) (Service from staff, info material, booking, shops, restaurants, wifi access etc.)

☐ Total (max 15p)

Ⓒ Capentum Förlag

Game activity

The most positive / negative with this golf club and its courses

Number of holes	Training with lighting	Driving range ok	Price worthy	Want to return
☐ 9 ☐ 18 ☐ 27 ☐ 36	☐ Yes ☐ No	☐ Yes ☐ No	☐ Yes ☐ No	☐ Yes ☐ No

Played from tee:	Winter greens	Handicap qualifying rounds possible	Open all year around
☐ White ☐ Yellow ☐ Blue ☐ Red	☐ Yes ☐ No	☐ Yes ☐ No	☐ Yes ☐ No

Date	Strokes	Scores	Played with:

Golf club

Name of the club:				Date	First visit
					Return visit

Address:				Lodging	Distance	Price
GPS:				Hotel ☐		
Website:				Cabin ☐		

Pay and Play ☐ Yes ☐ No	Short hole course ☐ Yes ☐ No	Name benefit card	Price	RV park ☐		
Golf package ☐ Yes ☐ No	Handigolf ☐ Yes ☐ No	Footgolf ☐ Yes ☐ No	Discount	Other ☐		

☐ Courses (1-5p) (Location, environment, maintenance, accessibility etc.)

☐ Facilities (1-5p) (Standard on toilets, showers, dressing room, lodging, parking etc.)

☐ Service (1-5p) (Service from staff, info material, booking, shops, restaurants, wifi access etc.)

☐ Total (max 15p)

© Capentum Förlag

Game activity

The most positive / negative with this golf club and its courses

Number of holes	Training with lighting	Driving range ok	Price worthy	Want to return
☐ 9 ☐ 18 ☐ 27 ☐ 36	☐ Yes ☐ No	☐ Yes ☐ No	☐ Yes ☐ No	☐ Yes ☐ No

Played from tee:	Winter greens	Handicap qualifying rounds possible	Open all year around
☐ White ☐ Yellow ☐ Blue ☐ Red	☐ Yes ☐ No	☐ Yes ☐ No	☐ Yes ☐ No

Date	Strokes	Scores	Played with:

Golf club

Name of the club:					Date	First visit		
						Return visit		
Address:					Lodging	Distance		Price
GPS:					Hotel ☐			
Website:					Cabin ☐			
Pay and Play ☐ Yes ☐ No	Short hole course ☐ Yes ☐ No	Name benefit card	Price		RV park ☐			
Golf package ☐ Yes ☐ No	Handigolf ☐ Yes ☐ No	Footgolf ☐ Yes ☐ No	Discount		Other ☐			

☐ Courses (1-5p) (Location, environment, maintenance, accessibility etc.)

☐ Facilities (1-5p) (Standard on toilets, showers, dressing room, lodging, parking etc.)

☐ Service (1-5p) (Service from staff, info material, booking, shops, restaurants, wifi access etc.)

☐ Total (max 15p)

© Capentum Förlag

Game activity

The most positive / negative with this golf club and its courses

Number of holes	Training with lighting	Driving range ok	Price worthy	Want to return
☐ 9 ☐ 18 ☐ 27 ☐ 36	☐ Yes ☐ No	☐ Yes ☐ No	☐ Yes ☐ No	☐ Yes ☐ No

Played from tee:	Winter greens	Handicap qualifying rounds possible	Open all year around
☐ White ☐ Yellow ☐ Blue ☐ Red	☐ Yes ☐ No	☐ Yes ☐ No	☐ Yes ☐ No

Date	Strokes	Scores	Played with:

Golf club

Name of the club:					Date	☐ First visit ☐ Return visit		
Address:					Lodging	Distance	Price	
GPS:					Hotel ☐			
Website:					Cabin ☐			
Pay and Play ☐ Yes ☐ No	Short hole course ☐ Yes ☐ No	Name benefit card	Price		RV park ☐			
Golf package ☐ Yes ☐ No	Handigolf ☐ Yes ☐ No	Footgolf ☐ Yes ☐ No	Discount		Other ☐			

☐ Courses (1-5p) (Location, environment, maintenance, accessibility etc.)

☐ Facilities   (1-5p) (Standard on toilets, showers, dressing room, lodging, parking etc.)

☐ Service (1-5p) (Service from staff, info material, booking, shops, restaurants, wifi access etc.)

☐ Total (max 15p)

© Capentum Förlag

Game activity

The most positive / negative with this golf club and its courses

Number of holes	Training with lighting	Driving range ok	Price worthy	Want to return
☐ 9 ☐ 18 ☐ 27 ☐ 36	☐ Yes ☐ No	☐ Yes ☐ No	☐ Yes ☐ No	☐ Yes ☐ No

Played from tee:	Winter greens	Handicap qualifying rounds possible	Open all year around
☐ White ☐ Yellow ☐ Blue ☐ Red	☐ Yes ☐ No	☐ Yes ☐ No	☐ Yes ☐ No

Date	Strokes	Scores	Played with:

Golf club

| Name of the club: | Date | ☐ First visit |
| | | ☐ Return visit |

		Lodging	Distance	Price
Address:				
GPS:		Hotel ☐		
Website:		Cabin ☐		

Pay and Play	Short hole course	Name benefit card	Price	RV park ☐		
☐ Yes ☐ No	☐ Yes ☐ No					
Golf package	Handigolf	Footgolf	Discount	Other ☐		
☐ Yes ☐ No	☐ Yes ☐ No	☐ Yes ☐ No				

☐ Courses (1-5p) (Location, environment, maintenance, accessibility etc.)

☐ Facilities (1-5p) (Standard on toilets, showers, dressing room, lodging, parking etc.)

☐ Service (1-5p) (Service from staff, info material, booking, shops, restaurants, wifi access etc.)

☐ Total (max 15p)

© Capentum Förlag

Game activity

The most positive / negative with this golf club and its courses

Number of holes	Training with lighting	Driving range ok	Price worthy	Want to return
☐ 9 ☐ 18 ☐ 27 ☐ 36	☐ Yes ☐ No	☐ Yes ☐ No	☐ Yes ☐ No	☐ Yes ☐ No

Played from tee:		Winter greens	Handicap qualifying rounds possible	Open all year around
☐ White ☐ Yellow ☐ Blue ☐ Red		☐ Yes ☐ No	☐ Yes ☐ No	☐ Yes ☐ No

Date	Strokes	Scores	Played with:

Golf club

Name of the club:					Date	First visit ☐		
						Return visit ☐		

Address:					Lodging	Distance	Price

GPS:					Hotel ☐		

Website:					Cabin ☐		

Pay and Play	Short hole course	Name benefit card	Price	RV park
☐ Yes ☐ No	☐ Yes ☐ No			☐

Golf package	Handigolf	Footgolf	Discount	Other
☐ Yes ☐ No	☐ Yes ☐ No	☐ Yes ☐ No		☐

☐ **Courses (1-5p)** (Location, environment, maintenance, accessibility etc.)

☐ **Facilities (1-5p)** (Standard on toilets, showers, dressing room, lodging, parking etc.)

☐ **Service (1-5p)** (Service from staff, info material, booking, shops, restaurants, wifi access etc.)

☐ **Total (max 15p)**

© Capentum Förlag

Game activity

The most positive / negative with this golf club and its courses

Number of holes				Training with lighting		Driving range ok		Price worthy		Want to return	
☐ 9	☐ 18	☐ 27	☐ 36	☐ Yes	☐ No	☐ Yes	☐ No	☐ Yes	☐ No	☐ Yes	☐ No

Played from tee:				Winter greens		Handicap qualifying rounds possible		Open all year around	
☐ White	☐ Yellow	☐ Blue	☐ Red	☐ Yes	☐ No	☐ Yes	☐ No	☐ Yes	☐ No

Date	Strokes	Scores	Played with:

Golf club

Name of the club:				Date	☐ First visit
					☐ Return visit

Address:				Lodging	Distance	Price
GPS:				Hotel ☐		
Website:				Cabin ☐		

Pay and Play ☐ Yes ☐ No	Short hole course ☐ Yes ☐ No	Name benefit card	Price	RV park ☐		
Golf package ☐ Yes ☐ No	Handigolf ☐ Yes ☐ No	Footgolf ☐ Yes ☐ No	Discount	Other ☐		

☐ **Courses (1-5p)** (Location, environment, maintenance, accessibility etc.)

☐ **Facilities** (1-5p) (Standard on toilets, showers, dressing room, lodging, parking etc.)

☐ **Service (1-5p)** (Service from staff, info material, booking, shops, restaurants, wifi access etc.)

☐ **Total** (max 15p)

© Capentum Förlag

Game activity

The most positive / negative with this golf club and its courses

Number of holes	Training with lighting	Driving range ok	Price worthy	Want to return
☐ 9 ☐ 18 ☐ 27 ☐ 36	☐ Yes ☐ No	☐ Yes ☐ No	☐ Yes ☐ No	☐ Yes ☐ No

Played from tee:	Winter greens	Handicap qualifying rounds possible	Open all year around
☐ White ☐ Yellow ☐ Blue ☐ Red	☐ Yes ☐ No	☐ Yes ☐ No	☐ Yes ☐ No

Date	Strokes	Scores	Played with:

Golf club

Name of the club:					Date	☐ First visit ☐ Return visit		
Address:					Lodging	Distance	Price	
GPS:					Hotel ☐			
Website:					Cabin ☐			
Pay and Play ☐ Yes ☐ No	Short hole course ☐ Yes ☐ No	Name benefit card		Price	RV park ☐			
Golf package ☐ Yes ☐ No	Handigolf ☐ Yes ☐ No	Footgolf ☐ Yes ☐ No		Discount	Other ☐			

☐ **Courses (1-5p)** (Location, environment, maintenance, accessibility etc.)

☐ **Facilities** **(1-5p)** (Standard on toilets, showers, dressing room, lodging, parking etc.)

☐ **Service** **(1-5p)** (Service from staff, info material, booking, shops, restaurants, wifi access etc.)

☐ **Total**
(max 15p)

© Capentum Förlag

Game activity

The most positive / negative with this golf club and its courses

Number of holes	Training with lighting	Driving range ok	Price worthy	Want to return
☐ 9 ☐ 18 ☐ 27 ☐ 36	☐ Yes ☐ No	☐ Yes ☐ No	☐ Yes ☐ No	☐ Yes ☐ No

Played from tee:	Winter greens	Handicap qualifying rounds possible	Open all year around
☐ White ☐ Yellow ☐ Blue ☐ Red	☐ Yes ☐ No	☐ Yes ☐ No	☐ Yes ☐ No

Date	Strokes	Scores	Played with:

Golf club

Name of the club:		Date	☐ First visit ☐ Return visit		
Address:		Lodging	Distance	Price
GPS:		Hotel ☐		
Website:		Cabin ☐		

Pay and Play ☐ Yes ☐ No	Short hole course ☐ Yes ☐ No	Name benefit card	Price	RV park ☐		
Golf package ☐ Yes ☐ No	Handigolf ☐ Yes ☐ No	Footgolf ☐ Yes ☐ No	Discount	Other ☐		

☐ Courses (1-5p) (Location, environment, maintenance, accessibility etc.)

☐ Facilities (1-5p) (Standard on toilets, showers, dressing room, lodging, parking etc.)

☐ Service (1-5p) (Service from staff, info material, booking, shops, restaurants, wifi access etc.)

☐ Total
(max
15p)

© Capentum Förlag

Game activity

The most positive / negative with this golf club and its courses

Number of holes	Training with lighting	Driving range ok	Price worthy	Want to return
☐ 9 ☐ 18 ☐ 27 ☐ 36	☐ Yes ☐ No	☐ Yes ☐ No	☐ Yes ☐ No	☐ Yes ☐ No

Played from tee:	Winter greens	Handicap qualifying rounds possible	Open all year around
☐ White ☐ Yellow ☐ Blue ☐ Red	☐ Yes ☐ No	☐ Yes ☐ No	☐ Yes ☐ No

Date	Strokes	Scores	Played with:

Golf club

Name of the club:					Date	☐ First visit ☐ Return visit		
Address:					Lodging	Distance	Price	
GPS:					Hotel ☐			
Website:					Cabin ☐			

Pay and Play ☐ Yes ☐ No	Short hole course ☐ Yes ☐ No	Name benefit card	Price	RV park ☐	
Golf package ☐ Yes ☐ No	Handigolf ☐ Yes ☐ No	Footgolf ☐ Yes ☐ No	Discount	Other ☐	

☐ Courses (1-5p) (Location, environment, maintenance, accessibility etc.)

☐ Facilities (1-5p) (Standard on toilets, showers, dressing room, lodging, parking etc.)

☐ Service (1-5p) (Service from staff, info material, booking, shops, restaurants, wifi access etc.)

☐ Total (max 15p)

© Capentum Förlag

Game activity

The most positive / negative with this golf club and its courses

Number of holes	Training with lighting	Driving range ok	Price worthy	Want to return
☐ 9 ☐ 18 ☐ 27 ☐ 36	☐ Yes ☐ No	☐ Yes ☐ No	☐ Yes ☐ No	☐ Yes ☐ No

Played from tee:	Winter greens	Handicap qualifying rounds possible	Open all year around
☐ White ☐ Yellow ☐ Blue ☐ Red	☐ Yes ☐ No	☐ Yes ☐ No	☐ Yes ☐ No

Date	Strokes	Scores	Played with:

Golf club

Name of the club:		Date	☐ First visit ☐ Return visit

Address:		Lodging	Distance	Price
GPS:		Hotel ☐		
Website:		Cabin ☐		

Pay and Play	Short hole course	Name benefit card	Price	RV park		
☐ Yes ☐ No	☐ Yes ☐ No			☐		
Golf package	Handigolf	Footgolf	Discount	Other		
☐ Yes ☐ No	☐ Yes ☐ No	☐ Yes ☐ No		☐		

☐ Courses (1–5p) (Location, environment, maintenance, accessibility etc.)

☐ Facilities (1–5p) (Standard on toilets, showers, dressing room, lodging, parking etc.)

☐ Service (1–5p) (Service from staff, info material, booking, shops, restaurants, wifi access etc.)

☐ Total
(max
15p)

© Capentum Förlag

Game activity

The most positive / negative with this golf club and its courses

Number of holes	Training with lighting	Driving range ok	Price worthy	Want to return
☐ 9 ☐ 18 ☐ 27 ☐ 36	☐ Yes ☐ No	☐ Yes ☐ No	☐ Yes ☐ No	☐ Yes ☐ No

Played from tee:	Winter greens	Handicap qualifying rounds possible	Open all year around
☐ White ☐ Yellow ☐ Blue ☐ Red	☐ Yes ☐ No	☐ Yes ☐ No	☐ Yes ☐ No

Date	Strokes	Scores	Played with:

Golf club

Name of the club:					Date	First visit ☐		
						Return visit ☐		
Address:						Lodging	Distance	Price
GPS:						Hotel ☐		
Website:						Cabin ☐		

Pay and Play	Short hole course	Name benefit card	Price	RV park
☐ Yes ☐ No	☐ Yes ☐ No			☐
Golf package	Handigolf	Footgolf	Discount	Other
☐ Yes ☐ No	☐ Yes ☐ No	☐ Yes ☐ No		☐

☐ Courses (1-5p) (Location, environment, maintenance, accessibility etc.)

☐ Facilities (1-5p) (Standard on toilets, showers, dressing room, lodging, parking etc.)

☐ Service (1-5p) (Service from staff, info material, booking, shops, restaurants, wifi access etc.)

☐ Total (max 15p)

© Capentum Förlag

Game activity

The most positive / negative with this golf club and its courses

Number of holes	Training with lighting	Driving range ok	Price worthy	Want to return
☐ 9 ☐ 18 ☐ 27 ☐ 36	☐ Yes ☐ No	☐ Yes ☐ No	☐ Yes ☐ No	☐ Yes ☐ No

Played from tee:	Winter greens	Handicap qualifying rounds possible	Open all year around
☐ White ☐ Yellow ☐ Blue ☐ Red	☐ Yes ☐ No	☐ Yes ☐ No	☐ Yes ☐ No

Date	Strokes	Scores	Played with:

Golf club

Name of the club:			Date	☐ First visit ☐ Return visit		
Address:			Lodging	Distance		Price
GPS:			Hotel ☐			
Website:			Cabin ☐			

Pay and Play ☐ Yes ☐ No	Short hole course ☐ Yes ☐ No	Name benefit card	Price	RV park ☐		
Golf package ☐ Yes ☐ No	Handigolf ☐ Yes ☐ No	Footgolf ☐ Yes ☐ No	Discount	Other ☐		

☐ Courses (1-5p) (Location, environment, maintenance, accessibility etc.)

☐ Facilities   (1-5p) (Standard on toilets, showers, dressing room, lodging, parking etc.)

☐ Service (1-5p) (Service from staff, info material, booking, shops, restaurants, wifi access etc.)

☐ Total
(max 15p)

© Capentum Förlag

Game activity

The most positive / negative with this golf club and its courses

Number of holes	Training with lighting	Driving range ok	Price worthy	Want to return
☐ 9 ☐ 18 ☐ 27 ☐ 36	☐ Yes ☐ No	☐ Yes ☐ No	☐ Yes ☐ No	☐ Yes ☐ No

Played from tee:		Winter greens	Handicap qualifying rounds possible	Open all year around
☐ White ☐ Yellow ☐ Blue ☐ Red		☐ Yes ☐ No	☐ Yes ☐ No	☐ Yes ☐ No

Date	Strokes	Scores	Played with:

Golf club

Name of the club:					Date	☐ First visit ☐ Return visit		

Address:					Lodging	Distance	Price

GPS:					Hotel ☐		

Website:					Cabin ☐		

Pay and Play ☐ Yes ☐ No	Short hole course ☐ Yes ☐ No	Name benefit card	Price	RV park ☐		

Golf package ☐ Yes ☐ No	Handigolf ☐ Yes ☐ No	Footgolf ☐ Yes ☐ No	Discount	Other ☐		

☐ Courses (1–5p) (Location, environment, maintenance, accessibility etc.)

☐ Facilities (1–5p) (Standard on toilets, showers, dressing room, lodging, parking etc.)

☐ Service (1–5p) (Service from staff, info material, booking, shops, restaurants, wifi access etc.)

☐ Total (max 15p)

© Capentum Förlag

Game activity

The most positive / negative with this golf club and its courses

Number of holes	Training with lighting	Driving range ok	Price worthy	Want to return
☐ 9 ☐ 18 ☐ 27 ☐ 36	☐ Yes ☐ No	☐ Yes ☐ No	☐ Yes ☐ No	☐ Yes ☐ No

Played from tee:	Winter greens	Handicap qualifying rounds possible	Open all year around
☐ White ☐ Yellow ☐ Blue ☐ Red	☐ Yes ☐ No	☐ Yes ☐ No	☐ Yes ☐ No

Date	Strokes	Scores	Played with:

Golf club

Name of the club:		Date	☐ First visit
			☐ Return visit

Address:		Lodging	Distance	Price
GPS:		Hotel ☐		
Website:		Cabin ☐		

Pay and Play ☐ Yes ☐ No	Short hole course ☐ Yes ☐ No	Name benefit card	Price	RV park ☐		
Golf package ☐ Yes ☐ No	Handigolf ☐ Yes ☐ No	Footgolf ☐ Yes ☐ No	Discount	Other ☐		

☐ Courses (1-5p) (Location, environment, maintenance, accessibility etc.)

☐ Facilities   (1-5p) (Standard on toilets, showers, dressing room, lodging, parking etc.)

☐ Service (1-5p) (Service from staff, info material, booking, shops, restaurants, wifi access etc.)

☐ Total (max 15p)

© Capentum Förlag

Game activity

The most positive / negative with this golf club and its courses

Number of holes				Training with lighting		Driving range ok		Price worthy		Want to return	
☐ 9 ☐ 18 ☐ 27 ☐ 36				☐ Yes ☐ No		☐ Yes ☐ No		☐ Yes ☐ No		☐ Yes ☐ No	

Played from tee:				Winter greens		Handicap qualifying rounds possible		Open all year around	
☐ White ☐ Yellow ☐ Blue ☐ Red				☐ Yes ☐ No		☐ Yes ☐ No		☐ Yes ☐ No	

Date	Strokes	Scores	Played with:

© Capentum Förlag

Golf club

| Name of the club: | Date | First visit ☐ |
| | | Return visit ☐ |

Name of the club:

	Date	First visit ☐ Return visit ☐

Address:

Lodging	Distance	Price

GPS:

| Hotel ☐ | | |

Website:

| Cabin ☐ | | |

Pay and Play ☐ Yes ☐ No	Short hole course ☐ Yes ☐ No	Name benefit card	Price	RV park ☐		
Golf package ☐ Yes ☐ No	Handigolf ☐ Yes ☐ No	Footgolf ☐ Yes ☐ No	Discount	Other ☐		

☐ Courses (1–5p) (Location, environment, maintenance, accessibility etc.)

☐ Facilities (1–5p) (Standard on toilets, showers, dressing room, lodging, parking etc.)

☐ Service (1–5p) (Service from staff, info material, booking, shops, restaurants, wifi access etc.)

☐ Total (max 15p)

© Capentum Förlag

Game activity

The most positive / negative with this golf club and its courses

Number of holes	Training with lighting	Driving range ok	Price worthy	Want to return
☐ 9 ☐ 18 ☐ 27 ☐ 36	☐ Yes ☐ No	☐ Yes ☐ No	☐ Yes ☐ No	☐ Yes ☐ No

Played from tee:	Winter greens	Handicap qualifying rounds possible	Open all year around
☐ White ☐ Yellow ☐ Blue ☐ Red	☐ Yes ☐ No	☐ Yes ☐ No	☐ Yes ☐ No

Date	Strokes	Scores	Played with: